Even a child
is known by his doings,
whether his work be pure,
and whether it be right.

Proverbs 20:11 KJV

# Little Lumpy's Book of Blessings

By L. Carol Lewis

Illustrations by Christopher B. Clarke

 Butterflies ENTERTAINMENT & PRESS

Published by Three Butterflies Entertainment and Press
130 Ryerson Street, Brooklyn, New York 11205

ISBN 0-9702415-0-X

Lewis, L. Carol
    Little Lumpy's book of blessings / by L. Carol
Lewis ; illustrations by Christopher B. Clarke. --
1st ed.
    SUMMARY: Little Lumpy talks about everything
for which she is thankful.
    Audience: Age 4-8.

    1.    Gratitude--Juvenile fiction.  I. Clarke,
Christopher B.  II. Title.

PZ7.L4956Li 2000          [E]
          QBI00-500032

Printed in Hong Kong

## In Memoriam

Ruth Louise Champion, Doris Kenyon Tucker, Delores Marie Clay,
The Figgs, Della Kibler, Ethel Mae Todd, Tracey Kenyon Tucker and

## My Dear Mother
## Thelma Lutisher Lewis

## Special Thanks

Cozette Wallace-Brewer, Ruby Iman Brewer, Joy Burton, Brenda Canty, Patricia Harris,

S. Alease Ferguson, Sharon A. Lewis and Harold Clayton Lewis

Yvonne Sims, LorRenne Norman, Walter R. Quick, Jr., Samuel Robinson,
Michelle Spillman, Kevin Strong and The Marsh-McLennan Bible Study, Lee & Debra,
Edith Washington, Mike A. Austin and

The Artist Almighty
Christopher B. Clarke

Hello! My name is Lia, but my mother calls me
Little Lumpy Lulu. You may call me Little Lumpy, for short.

This is my book of blessings. Blessings are things that are good for us, things for which we are thankful.

I am so thankful and there are many reasons why. Let me show you.

Mommy and Daddy make me feel so special. They work so hard to give me a lovely home.

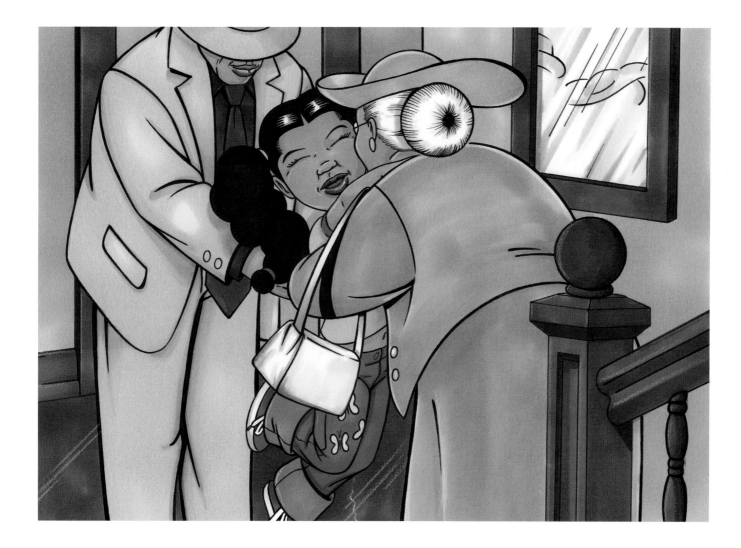

Not only do I have Mommy and Daddy,
but I have Grandma and Grandpa too.
Grandma and Grandpa give me big hugs and kisses.

I enjoy holidays and family gatherings. My aunts, uncles and cousins come over to our house for a jolly time.

I am thankful for my sitter, Mrs. Todd. She teaches me all kinds of things, like how to do puzzles, play checkers and make cookies.

I am thankful
for my playmates,
Precious P.J.,
Amazing, Hector,
LingoLingo, Hazel
and Asher. We
have lots of fun.

Then there
is Puggles,
my puppy.
Puggles makes
me happy when
I am sad.

Puggles sometimes gets into
Mommy's garden of beautiful flowers.

Daddy planted a blueberry bush
just for me next to Mommy's garden.

Mommy and Daddy built a sandbox in our backyard so that I can build sandcastles with my friends.

I am thankful for training wheels.
Training wheels allow us to go faster and faster.

We can go fast because we eat fruits and vegetables that make us strong and healthy.

If we do not eat healthy foods
we get sick and cannot go outside.

Except to
visit the doctor
and nurse who
help make us
healthy again.

When I am better I can go out and play in the warm sun. The sun chases the clouds away and brings us bright, warm days.

When the sun is too hot, I sit under
a big green leafy tree for cool shade.

I am thankful
for nature.
Nature is
the perfect
setting for
outings.

When the day comes to an end, Mommy and Daddy read a bedtime story to me.

The moon and the stars keep me company after I fall asleep and Mommy and Daddy kiss me goodnight.

Before I go, I must tell you something. I am thankful for my latest blessing, you my new friend. Goodnight!

# Dedication

## To The Children of The World,

Whatever your hand finds to do, do it with all your might; I have seen something else under the sun: The race is not to the swift or the battle to the strong, nor does food come to the wise or wealth to the brilliant or favor to the learned; but time and chance happen to them all.

Ecclesiastes 9:10a,11, from the New International Version (NIV)

L. Carol Lewis is a literary entrepreneur serving as Founder and Chief Executive Officer of Three Butterflies Entertainment & Press. She is a graduate of Bowling Green State University and Howard University School of Law where she served as Managing Editor of the Howard Law Journal (1994 – 1995) and received the Fats Waller Award for Excellence in Entertainment Law (1995). *Little Lumpy's Book of Blessings* is L. Carol's triumphant gift to the world. This labor of love is intended to bless children, families and all of humanity by gently conveying the enduring message of God's love and the many, yet simple manifestations of His anointing, grace and mercy. In producing this publication L. Carol was driven by the truth that "[f]or unto whomsoever much is given, of him shall be much required: and to whom men have committed much, of him they will ask more." Luke 12:48 KJV. Diligently seeking to be a faithful steward, L. Carol presents this inceptive and remarkably beautiful and thoughtful volume for your enjoyment and edification. To God be all the glory!

Christopher B. Clarke has always been recognized for his talent as an artist. This Brooklyn-born and bred Bedford-Stuyvesant resident cherishes early memories of exhibiting outstanding artistic abilities. Many of his accomplishments have stemmed from competitions and awards like the prestigious Haney Award from the New York Art League (1987) for artistic excellence, which he received during his second year at the High School of Art and Design. Since graduating from Pratt Institute in 1994 with a BEA in Communication Design, Christopher has free-

lanced and worked in-house as a storyboard and comprehensive illustrator at various advertisement agencies and record companies. He has contributed cover art for several notable African-American novels such as Omar Tyree's For the Love of Money, Deloroys Welch-Tyson's Gingersnaps and High Hand by Gary Philips. While maintaining high artistic standards and professionalism on a variety of unique assignments, Chris brings these same attributes to *Little Lumpy's Book of Blessings.* He is committed to this high mark, particularly in relation to every artistic element of *Little Lumpy* (created by L. Carol Lewis and produced by Three Butterflies Entertainment & Press).

Walter Quick Jr. is the co-founder of Kingdom By Design, a multi-discipline art direction and design firm created to serve the needs of the Kingdom of God. The book design for *Little Lumpy's Book of Blessings* was one of God's great opportunities for Walter to invest his creative talent. He established his interest in design at The Phillippa Schyler School for the Gifted and Talented, the High School of Art & Design, and the Fashion Institute for Technology (SUNY). He has worked over eight years, from New York to Los Angeles, as an art director and graphic designer in music, publishing, television, and film. Walter resides in Los Angles, California with his wife and business partner, Phylicia.